THE BOOK OF Flies

Matt Reher   April Ferry

This is a fly.

All flies have eyes.

antennae
Flies smell with their antennae, like humans smell with a nose.

All flies have these.

European Hoverfly

Mydas Fly

Marmalade Hoverfly

There are lots of flies.

This is a house.

Musca domestica

This is a house fly.

House flies have tiny hairs on the bottom of their legs that they use to taste whatever they land on.

They have lots of hair.

This is fruit.

Fruit flies get their name from their attraction to rotting vegetables and fruits.

Drosophila melanogaster

This is a fruit fly.

Fruit flies are yellow.

They have big red eyes.

This is sand.

Sand flies have very hairy wings.

wing hair

Sand flies get their name from their sandy brown color, but they also live in sandy areas.

Phlebotominae

This is a sand fly.

17

Sand flies are so small that they are hard to see. They are only 3mm long, about half the length of a mosquito.

3 mm   6 mm

18 **Sand flies are little.**

They have big legs.

This is a horse.

This is a horse fly.

Tabanidae

Horse flies can be black or brown.

They have big green eyes. 23

COSTA RICA

PENNSYLVANIA

24 Can you see all the flies?

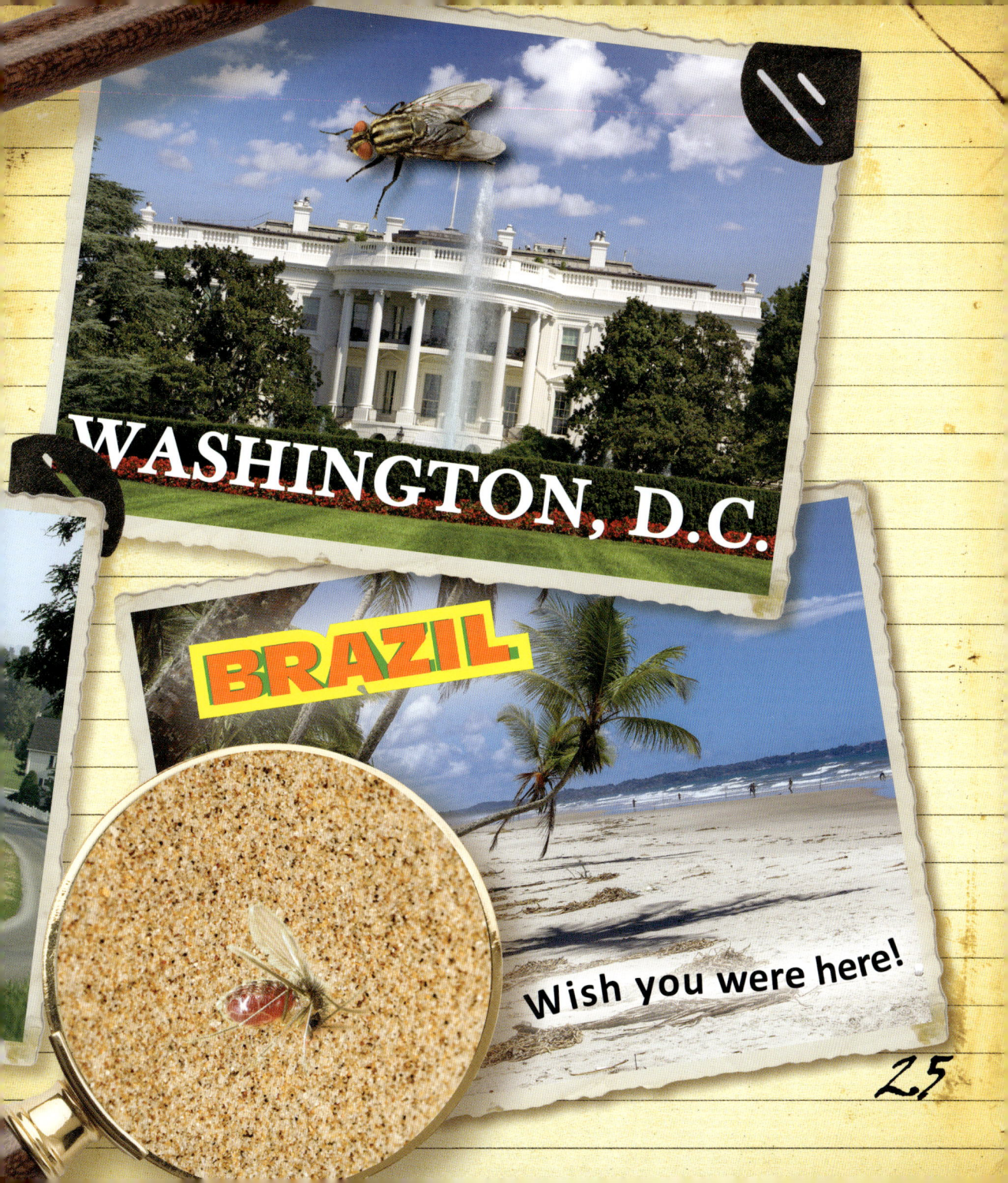

Can you match the word to the color?

black

green

red

yellow

Is that a fly?

Some flies look like other insects to avoid predators. The long hoverfly looks like a wasp, but it's not! It is a fly. Unlike a wasp, it has no stinger.

← fly

Long Hoverfly

Paper Wasp

← not a fly

Flies also have short antennae and big heads and eyes. Wasps can have very long or curly antennae and smaller heads.

27

Matching Challenge

I can use the first letter sound to match the word to the picture.

wing

horse

fly

sand